THE ROMANS

Peter Hicks

Wayland

Look into the Past

Series editor: Joanna Housley
Series designer: David West
Book designer: Joyce Chester

First published in 1993 by Wayland (Publishers) Ltd,
61 Western Road, Hove, East Sussex, BN3 1JD, England

British Library Cataloguing in Publication Data
Hicks, Peter
Romans. – (Look into the Past series)
I. Title II. Series
937

ISBN 0 7502 0820 1

Typeset by Dorchester Typesetting Group Ltd.,
Dorset, England.
Printed and bound in Italy by L.E.G.O. S.p.A.,
Vicenza, Italy.

Picture acknowledgements
The publishers wish to thank the following for supplying the
photographs for this book: Canterbury Heritage Museum 29
(top); C M Dixon 5 (top), 7 (bottom), 8 (both), 9 (top), 11
(bottom), 12, 13 (right), 17 (top), 18, 19 (bottom), 20, 21
(all), 23 (both), 25 (both), 26 (top); English Heritage 19
(top); Focal Point 9 (bottom), 10, 11 (top), 16, 24; Sonia
Halliday 29 (bottom); Robert Harding 6, 14, 15 (top), 17
(bottom), 22; Peter Hicks 13 (bottom left), 15 (bottom), 27;
The Mansell Collection 28; Wayland 4; Werner Forman
Archive 26 (bottom).
Map artwork by Jenny Hughes.

CONTENTS

Words that appear in **bold italic** in the text are explained in the glossary on page 30.

WHO WERE THE ROMANS?

The story of Rome, its people and the *empire* they built is both impressive and exciting. From a city built on the banks of the River Tiber in central Italy sprang a mighty empire that stretched into three continents and lasted nearly 700 years. The Romans built lasting roads, bridges and towns. They produced great literature and art, strong government, and a powerful army and navy. However, Roman rule could be very cruel. The Roman army fought many battles and conquered huge areas. They often treated prisoners of war and *civilians* very badly. Also, we must not forget that the whole Roman way of life was based on millions of *slaves* doing most of the work. Many slaves led lives of misery.

▼ The beginning of Rome is wrapped up in *legend*. It is said that two young brothers, Romulus and Remus, were abandoned on the banks of the River Tiber. A she-wolf appeared from the forest, suckled them and saved them from starvation. The statue here shows this famous event. Can you see the baby brothers feeding? The legend tells us that they were brought up by a shepherd and his kind wife. When he was a young man, Romulus founded Rome with the help of the gods. He ploughed a trench in the shape of the new city, but then killed his brother Remus in a fight for the throne. The story – perhaps a way of telling the Romans that they were special – was said to have happened in 753 BC.

Archaeologists ▶ have discovered that nearly 4,000 years ago a tribe called the Latini were settled and farming in the region where Rome was built. The land was very *fertile* and the weather was good, so crops grew well. Farmers grew grain and vegetables and raised animals. The picture shows a ploughman with his team of oxen which would have worked the fields. The Latini were simple people living in thatched huts. It is believed their small farms gradually developed into villages and towns.

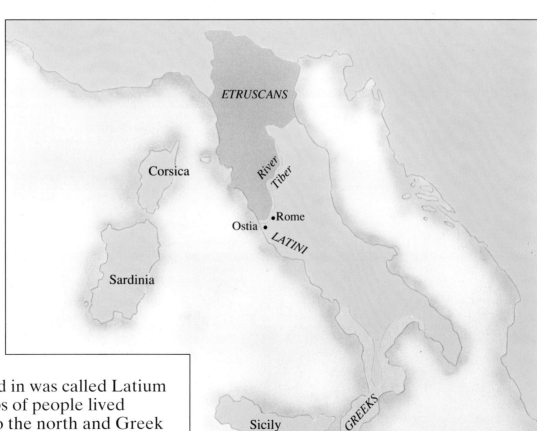

The area the Latini lived in was called Latium and two powerful groups of people lived nearby: the Etruscans to the north and Greek settlers to the south. The Latini traded with these people and it is not surprising that they picked up many ideas from them, such as the use of the alphabet. In fact, many of the ideas that made the Roman Empire so great came from the Etruscans and Greeks.

THE GROWTH OF AN EMPIRE

The cluster of tribal settlements that came together to form the city of Rome was situated on a group of hills above the River Tiber. The high ground and river protected Rome from enemy attack. The city was also 24 km upstream from the Mediterranean Sea, which meant it was unlikely to be attacked by pirates roaming the Mediterranean. But it was not too far from the sea for Roman traders to reach the sea routes. Below the hills, the Tiber narrows, making an excellent bridging point for travellers and traders. It is not surprising that, in such a good position, Rome grew quickly.

▲ One problem Rome faced was lowland flooding near the Tiber. Once this area was successfully drained, it was made into an open space for meetings called the forum, the remains of which you can see in the picture. The city council met in a building called the curia at the forum. People also went to the forum to trade goods and to listen to speeches.

Rome had to deal with several attacks by her neighbours before becoming a strong empire. But by 146 BC Rome controlled all the trade in the Mediterranean and felt strong enough to expand. The Roman army conquered the Greeks to the east and moved north and west.

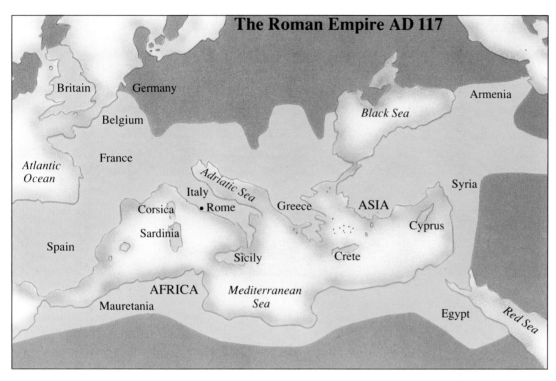

The Roman Empire AD 117

Britain
Germany
Belgium
France
Atlantic Ocean
Italy
Corsica • Rome
Sardinia
Spain
Sicily
AFRICA
Mauretania
Mediterranean Sea
Adriatic Sea
Greece
Black Sea
Armenia
ASIA
Syria
Cyprus
Crete
Egypt
Red Sea

◄ Look carefully at the map of the Roman Empire. Can you see the land that Rome conquered? Every time they defeated a tribe, they set up a province. When a new province was brought into the empire, all its wealth and goods were taken out. These would be grain, animals, wine, money through taxes, or valuable metals such as iron, lead or gold, or human beings sold as slaves.

Look at the carvings on this column in ▶ Rome. They show the Roman army capturing a **barbarian** village. It is a shocking scene – men are being killed, homes are being destroyed, as an old man prays to his gods for help. A woman and child try to escape, but a soldier pulls the woman back by the hair. What will happen to them? They will be taken prisoner and sold as slaves. After a war, slaves were plentiful and cheap, and many rich Romans bought them. Some masters looked after their slaves well, but many slaves were treated cruelly and **branded** like animals on the forehead or leg, as the property of their owners.

7

▼ By AD 100, with all the wealth pouring into Rome from the Empire, the city was the largest and most impressive in the world, with a million people living there. Look at the model of Rome. It gives us a good idea of what the city would have looked like.

You have probably noticed how crowded it was with houses, flats, public baths and shops. Can you see the huge Colosseum on the right and the Circus Maximus in the foreground? These buildings were where the Roman Games took place.

◄ Huge amounts of grain were needed for the large population and Rome, therefore, depended on plentiful amounts coming in from the Empire. Free grain was given out to the poor and, if this ran out, riots would often take place. This *mosaic* shows a man measuring corn, a vital crop for the Romans.

By AD 100 the ▶
Roman Empire was a
huge area with an
emperor at its head.
The Empire was
linked by an
impressive network of
roads. Many Roman
roads were long and
straight. Why was
this? Straight roads
allowed troops to
travel quickly and
directly to any
troublespots in the
Empire. Many of
these straight roads
built by the Romans
still exist today.

◀ The Romans also
built roads to cross
mountains. Can you
see the road twisting
and turning over the
Alps? This was built
by the Romans and
shows what excellent
engineers they were.

THE ARMY

The Roman Empire would never have grown had it not been for the efficient army. We know a lot about the army, because its troops went to many places and left behind a lot of evidence of their presence. The Roman army was divided into huge groups called legions. A legion could contain up to 6,000 soldiers. In the early days of the Roman Empire, soldiers were part-timers, which meant they only fought when they were needed. As the size of the Empire increased the soldiers were employed full-time. When men joined the army they had to stay for twenty five years!

The best trained, ▶ best equipped and highest paid Roman soldier was the legionary. The only people who could become legionaries were Roman *citizens* or the sons of legionaries. In the picture you can see a small group of them. Can you see their helmets, spears and rectangular shields? The shields were used for attack as well as defence. Legionaries not only had to fight, but they were also expected to be good builders and engineers. When not fighting, they were expected to build camps, forts, roads,

bridges and walls.

◀ In the picture you can see one example of the evidence left behind by Roman soldiers. When the army attacked Maiden Castle in England in AD 43, they shot one of the defenders with a ballista bolt – a heavy arrow shot from a crossbow. When the site was *excavated* by archaeologists they found his body, with the iron tip of the arrow still in one of the bones in his spine!

▼ This picture shows a section from Trajan's Column, which tells the story of the war against a tribe called the Dacias. The legionaries are hard at work. What are they doing? They are busy constructing a fort. Ditches are being dug, and fort walls and timber fences are being built.

▼ The two soldiers on guard with the round shields were called auxiliaries. They were recruited into the army from the tribes conquered by the Romans. By doing this, Roman customs were passed on to people in the areas that were conquered. The main job of the auxiliaries was to support the legions in battle. In fact, auxiliaries were often sent into the front line during a battle and many of them would be killed or wounded. Because they were not Roman citizens they were not valued as highly as legionaries.

Another important ▶ job the auxiliaries had was to man the forts and walls that protected the borders of the Empire. Look at the picture. You are standing on Hadrian's Wall, which for most of the time was the northernmost point of the Roman Empire. Although built by the legions by order of the Emperor Hadrian in AD 122, it was manned by auxiliary troops and acted as a barrier against the troublesome tribes of northern Britain. Can you see how it hugs the hills and crags? It was an amazing engineering feat, joining the east and west coasts of Britain.

A number of forts were built along Hadrian's Wall. At one called Housteads you can see an unusual building. It is the toilet block used by the soldiers! The two narrow channels are where the men washed their sponges to clean themselves – we use toilet paper. The block shows how well organized these forts were. ▶

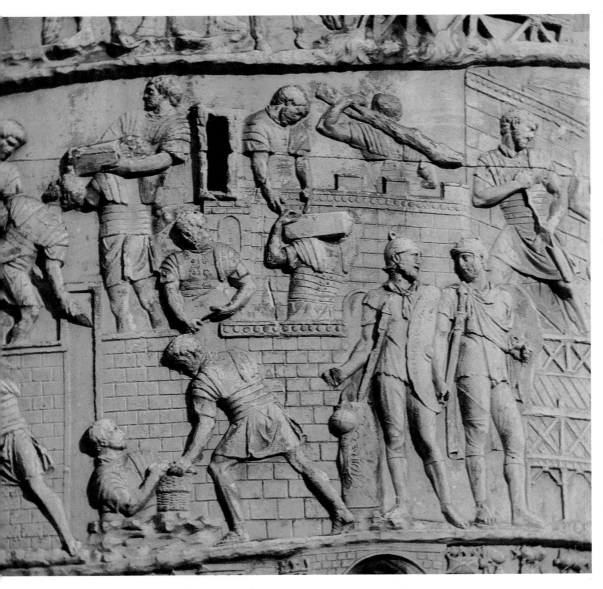

A great source of information about the army comes from the many soldiers' tombstones that have been found around the Empire. Because they did not want to be forgotten if they died far away from home, soldiers paid into a fund for a tombstone after their death. Look at the one in the picture. What can we learn from it? The stone shows a very important rank of soldier – a **centurion** from the 20th legion (one of the legions that built Hadrian's Wall). Can you see his armour? A centurion was in charge of eighty legionaries, often a difficult job. To show his rank he carried a staff, which he often used to hit his unruly legionaries! ▼

13

TOWN LIFE

Towns were very important in the growth of the Roman Empire, for they were a good way of spreading Roman ideas. The hundreds of towns in the Empire acted as centres of trade, religion, entertainment and learning. They were also centres of local government, and provided protection in times of danger. In the towns of the Empire, the local population could see Roman *architecture,* fashion, laws, sports and *hygiene.* This encouraged them to be good Romans.

Romans had very high standards of hygiene and the ***sewage systems*** in their towns were remarkable. They made sure there was a plentiful supply of clean water. As rivers and streams in towns were often polluted, a clean water spring was located – often a long way from town – and an ***aqueduct*** was built along which the water was carried. The picture shows part of the aqueduct that supplied water to Nîmes in France. Striding dramatically across a valley, this aqueduct carried pure water from 40 km away.

Most water was used for washing and ▶ drinking. It was supplied to fountains and the excess water was used to flush out the drains. More importantly, the water was used to feed the public baths built near the town forum. Romans loved to bathe daily and were very clean – they would be shocked by our standards of cleanliness! Bathing often took place after work when people visited the public baths on the way home. They were very cheap and the bath houses provided wine, food and entertainment. Look at the Roman baths at Bath in England. Although everything above the bases of the pillars was added in the nineteenth century, it is easy to imagine bathers chatting and drinking on the edge or jumping in.

Bathing houses ◀ were heated by a **_furnace_** and **_hypocaust system_**. The hot air from the furnace was channelled into an area under a floor supported by pillars. Can you see this in the picture? This made the room very hot, so the bathers would sweat before taking their bath. The hypocaust could also heat houses, which was very useful in cold parts of the Empire like Gaul (present-day France) and Britain! Look carefully and you can see the air channels at the side of the walls.

We know a lot about Roman towns from the exciting archaeological discoveries at Pompeii and Herculaneum, near Naples in Italy. Both towns were lost after the volcano Vesuvius erupted in AD 79, covering the towns in layers of volcanic mud, ash and lava. For centuries they lay forgotten, until the area was carefully uncovered, and the results were amazing. Streets, houses, *artefacts*, shops, bakeries, bars, barbers shops and laundries were preserved exactly as they were on the day the volcano erupted.

▲ Look at the wine bar with the jars still perfectly in place. These kept the wine cool – can you imagine a busy lunchtime full of drinkers having a snack of beans or lentils? Pompeii had at least 120 such bars!

◀ Poor people in Roman towns lived in small blocks of flats, but the rich could afford fine stone town houses with tiled roofs and these tend to be better preserved. Many had luxurious rooms, bath suites, mosaic floors and beautiful gardens. The one you see is at a house in Herculaneum.

Because ▶ archaeologists have found many artefacts they have been able to reconstruct the rooms they came from. This is a typical town house kitchen. The large storage containers are called amphorae, and you can see a large cooking pot and the oven.

COUNTRY LIFE

Our knowledge of the countryside in the Roman Empire is not as complete as that of the towns. What life was like for peasant farmers and slaves living in outlying settlements is less certain. We do know that farming was very important because enough food had to be produced to feed the huge Roman army and the millions of town and city dwellers. Life was very hard for people in the countryside – they worked all day in the fields, or cleared forests or laboured in mines and quarries.

In the Roman Empire good farming land was divided up into estates. Some were owned by rich tribal farmers who had become Romans, while others rented them from landlords. Many estates were owned by the emperor himself. Archaeologists have discovered that at the heart of these estates were large villas. Villa in Latin means farm, so it refers to the farm estates as well as the country home. Look at the mosaic of a north African estate with the villa at its centre. Can you work out some of the activities of this wealthy estate?

At one time archaeologists tended to concentrate only on villa buildings, but recently they have learned a lot more about the estates as a whole. Villas were the successful results of well-organized farming. The profits from the farming helped pay for villas that were luxuriously built and extended. This villa was enlarged to include heated rooms, bath suites and a mosaic-floored dining room.

This mosaic comes ▶ from a country villa in north Africa. A banquet is taking place. Can you see the man in the middle serving food? The guests are being entertained with music while they eat. What instrument is the man in the bottom right playing?

APPEARANCE

We tend to think of all Romans wearing the toga, but it was such a complicated piece of clothing that by the time of the Empire, it was mainly worn only for special ceremonies by wealthy citizens. Most poorer people usually wore simple woollen tunics with holes for the arms and head, held in at the waist by a belt.

The men on this carving are wearing togas. Made of wool or silk, the toga had to be three times the length of the wearer and was wrapped around the body leaving the right arm uncovered. During cold weather a heavy woollen cloak was worn over it.

Look at this Roman couple. Notice the ▶ woman's ringlets and hairband. She is holding a writing pen called a stylus and a writing tablet made of wax. With the stylus she would cut letters into a wax 'page'. Her husband wears his hair short, although it is also curled. This was done by a hairdresser with curling tongs. It was fashionable for men to wear perfume and face paint. Beards went in and out of fashion – if you look carefully you can see the man has a faint, wispy beard.

Jewellery was very popular amongst the wealthy, especially bronze and gold. Earrings and bracelets were highly decorated and very expensive.

ENTERTAINMENT

Because life was hard in Roman times, people living in the Empire loved entertainment. It was said that the only things Romans were interested in were entertainment and food! If you lived near a town or city there was a very good chance of regular entertainment in either the theatres or *arenas* built in the big settlements. Emperors realized that one way of remaining popular with the people of Rome was to provide free shows. These were known as the Roman Games. Men, often slaves, were specially trained as gladiators to fight to the death in the arena. Other shows included men fighting wild animals, chariot races, animal hunts and even sea battles (they had to flood the arena)!

◀ The first arena – or amphitheatre – was built around 53 BC. The most famous amphitheatre was the Colosseum in Rome, which you can see in the picture. Can you see how the crowds would have been seated on the raised tiers? Below the level of the floor you can still see the cells and corridors where the wild animals and gladiators waited until they were called to fight. Above them would have been 50,000 noisy spectators.

▼ One of the most popular spectator sports in the Empire was chariot racing, which you can see taking place in the carving below. The reason for its popularity was its great danger. Teams of charioteers would race at high speed, pushing and bumping each other as they went. One trick was to deliberately smash into the opposing chariots, hoping to destroy them. When this happened, the charioteer was 'shipwrecked' and he had to cut the reins quickly or risk being dragged by his own horses to death or serious injury. In Rome these races took place at the Circus Maximus, which could hold 250,000 spectators. By our standards these sports were very violent – most involved humans and animals in acts of great cruelty. However, their popularity shows how brutal and cheap life was in those days.

▲ Gladiators took part in fights against each other and against wild beasts. The Roman audience loved to watch men fighting to the death. Gladiators could not usually expect to live for longer than two or three fights in the arena, although sometimes a defeated man was allowed to live. If a gladiator did manage to win five fights in a row he was rewarded with his freedom.

23

GODS AND BURIAL

The Romans believed in many gods and they allowed different kinds of religious worship within their Empire. They drew the line at human sacrifice and this explains why Druidism – the religion of many *Iron Age* tribes – was brutally crushed by the army. The main Roman religion involved the belief that the emperor was a god. The three major Roman gods and goddesses were Jupiter, Juno and Minerva. They had a special temple on the most sacred hill in Rome, the Capitol.

◀ The painted statue shows the third most important goddess, Minerva. She was the goddess of wisdom, healing and arts and crafts.

Worship not only ▶ took place in temples – many people also had **shrines** in their homes to honour the local gods. This late Roman carving in ivory shows a woman making an offering at a shrine.

SYMMACHORVM

▼ The Romans were very suspicious of Christianity, because Christians did not believe the emperor could be a god. As a result Christians were often treated very cruelly. However, after the Emperor Constantine became a Christian in AD 324, Christianity spread to many parts of the Empire. This baptism pool was found in a Roman temple that was converted to an early Christian church in Tunisia.

The Romans also ▶ took in a number of religions from the Middle East. One, called Mithraism, was a secret and mysterious religion practised only by men. In a legend, the god Mithras had to kill a bull, whose blood had life-giving properties. This religion was very popular with soldiers, and a Mithraic Temple was built close to Hadrian's Wall.

◀ Roman law was very strict concerning the burial of the dead. Burials were not allowed inside towns and cities (except for babies) and **cemeteries** had to be outside city boundaries. Rich people were buried in tombs. In the picture you can see some tombs on the left. Poor people who were **cremated** had their ashes either buried or placed in pots. You can see some of these in the grass in front of the tombs.

THE FALL OF ROME

By the third century AD tribes outside the Roman Empire began raiding provinces in the hope of taking rich pickings. In response to this threat the boundaries of the Empire were strengthened and some cities built walls or added turrets to them. Around the coasts of Gaul and Britain special forts were built to watch out for Anglo-Saxon raiders, who came in longships from what is now Germany.

In the picture you can see one of these forts. Notice the huge towers that helped defenders see along their walls as well as improve their fire power. Can you also see the defensive ditch in front of the towers? 1,700 years ago this would have been much deeper.

As the attacks on ▶ the Empire continued, it became very difficult to collect taxes: people either refused to pay or could not afford to. This meant that the army could not be paid, so many soldiers ran off, leaving the Empire undefended. Once the army left, the Roman way of life collapsed remarkably quickly. Buildings were deserted, *pillaged*, burnt or left in ruins. Look at the picture of a once proud Roman city. People are living in clusters in the ruins. Can you see the large ruin in the centre? It was the theatre. Look at the city walls – crumbling and unmanned.
(On display in Canterbury Heritage Museum ©.)

▲ By the fifth century AD tribes from central Europe – the Franks, Vandals, Goths and Huns – were making serious inroads into Roman territory. One of these tribes, the Huns, was led by Attila, whom you can see on the medal. The Romans called these tribes barbarians because they lived outside the Empire and were not 'civilized'. The writing on the medal calls Attila the '*Scourge* of God'.

What does this tell us about him?

The Roman ▶
Empire was very
powerful while it was
growing. Defending
the frontier proved to
be much harder. By
AD 476 the Empire
had broken up. The
Eastern Empire,
based around
Constantinople (now
Istanbul in Turkey),
survived until the
fifteenth century.
You can see
Constantinople's large
city wall here. But the
once mighty Western
Empire lay in ruins.

GLOSSARY

Aqueduct A bridge for carrying water.

Archaeologists People who study objects and remains from the past.

Architecture The design and style of buildings.

Arena A place with seats around an open space where games or contests are held.

Artefacts Objects, such as tools or pots, that archaeologists study to find out how people used to live.

Barbarian The Romans called all tribespeople who lived outside the Empire barbarians. According to the Romans they were 'uncivilized', because they did not speak Latin or Greek.

Branded Stamped with a hot iron.

Cemeteries Places where dead people are buried.

Centurion A Roman soldier who was in charge of a group of eighty legionaries (called a century).

Citizens Members of a state or country who must obey its government and laws, and who have certain rights.

Civilians Ordinary members of the public, who are not in the army.

Cremated When a body has been burnt to ashes.

Empire A group of countries or states under one ruler.

Engineers People who design and make buildings, machines, roads and bridges.

Excavated Dug up buried ruins.

Fertile A word describing land that is good for farming because it is rich in the nutrients that plants need to help them grow.

Furnace A structure, like a very big oven, that can produce great heat.

Hygiene Clean or healthy practices.

Hypocaust system The Romans' way of heating buildings by spreading hot air beneath the floor.

Iron Age The period, which began in about 1100 BC, when iron began to be used widely.

Legend A story handed down from earlier times.

Mosaic A design made by arranging lots of small pieces of marble, stone, etc.

Pillaged Robbed a town during a war.

Scourge Someone who causes destruction.

Sewage system A system to carry off water and waste matter from buildings.

Shrines Places of worship.

Slaves People who are owned by and forced to work for other people.

IMPORTANT DATES

BC

c 753	Rome founded
c 507	Roman Republic starts
312	First Roman aqueduct completed
146	Carthage destroyed. Romans control the Mediterranean Sea
51	Gaul (mainly France) becomes part of the Roman Empire
27	Augustus becomes the first Roman Emperor
c 4	Birth of Jesus Christ

AD

43	Britain invaded and conquered
79	Eruption of Vesuvius – Pompeii and Herculaneum destroyed
113	Trajan's Column built
122	Hadrian's Wall in Britain built
293	Roman Empire split into east and west under two emperors
323	Emperor Constantine becomes a Christian
360	Picts and Scots cross Hadrian's Wall
455	Vandals sack Rome
476	Western Roman Empire destroyed

BOOKS TO READ

The Romans by Jacqueline Dineen (Heinemann Children's Reference, 1991) Examines the culture and history of the Romans.

See Inside a Roman Town by Jonathan Rutland (Kingfisher, 1986) Using cut-away illustrations, this book shows what life was like in a Roman town.

What do we know about the Romans? by Mike Corbishley (Simon & Schuster, 1991) This book answers questions about the Romans' everyday life using photographs and illustrations.

Living in Roman Times by Jane Chisholm (Usborne, 1982) This book describes the everyday life of the Romans, through a central character.

Roman Cities by Roger Coote (Wayland, 1990) This book concentrates on city life during Roman times, using artwork illustrations.

The Romans by Mike Corbishley (Kingfisher, 1992) The Roman period is vividly reconstructed using archaeological evidence.

INDEX